The Way Things Are

Roan McAuley

BookLeaf
Publishing

Presentation by *BookLeaf Publishing*

Web: www.bookleafpub.com

E-mail: info@bookleafpub.com

ISBN: 9789395969826

First edition 2022

The Beginning

When you wake,
Your day begins,
And another chapter
Of your journey is written.
Written as a small piece of your tale.

The same wind as yesterday
Blows through your hair,
And you hope that it blows
In a different direction than before,
Gently pushing your ship into new waters to sail.

The same sun as yesterday,
Shines down on your face.
Yet it feels just as warm
As it embraces your unguarded soul,
Never wavering in its carefree calling.

The same faces as yesterday
Gaze back at you,
Reflecting all of the light
And letting all of the dark
Drift down towards the deep, ever falling.

The same day as yesterday
Happens before your eyes,
Under your watch,
As golden as you remember it
Overflowing with both joy and strife.

How you spend your days
Is how you spend your life.

The Fan

Cool breeze,
Pressing upon my face.
A center without a middle.
A deep breath;
A cool breeze.

Cool breeze,
Blowing my hair to the right.
Asymmetrical comfort.
A sense of focus;
A cool breeze.

Cool breeze,
Radiating created wind.
An artificial companion.
A device with no other goal;
A cool breeze.

Cool Breeze,
Spinning in circles.
Yet moving forward.
A sense of purpose;
A cool breeze.

Time

The clock is always spinning,
Spinning in endless circles.
In spirals, you could say.
The only question is,
Which way?

On the days where your heart
Steams in its own humid fatigue,
Downwards it seems the spiral falls,
Spinning and falling and weeping,
Until the promise of a new day calls.

On the days where sunlight smiles
And laughs alongside you,
Upwards it seems the spiral spins,
Fearlessly climbing to the stars.
And it's at life that your soul wins.

On the days where the clouds
Slowly pass by your gaze,
The spiral spins without motion
And your mind wanders free,
Without thought, care, or notion.

And time stops.

But the clock keeps spinning.

Leap of Faith

Sometimes it's nice to know
That not everything is slow
And the great leap of faith will be done
After a moment of time that's practically none.
But I still hesitate to go.

Wouldn't it be less pain
To stay in my chain,
Knowing what the worst could be.
I'd rather forfeit all future glee
Than meet my own bane.

But would it be cheating
To simply not play the game?

And yet, the chance
To win at life's dance,
To have the dice roll in my favor
And let me be my own savior,
Is compelling me to risk the expanse.

But if time is really fleeting,
Why shouldn't I raise my name?

If determined is one's fate,
Then no one should debate
My own ambition.
My own expedition.
So I leap. And I wait.

That Thing I Should Really Do And Am Ready To Do But Just Don't Feel Like It - An Ode to Procrastination

Oh, omnipotent Procrastination,
Your strength impossible to diminish,
It even makes writing poetry
Impossible to

Back to the Normal

Sometimes you don't have to travel through time
To visit a memory from the distant past.
Sometimes to relive the sublime
You need to remember that then will last.

Your future self is gazing
Upon you, now, and
What is then, then,
Is now, now.

The Dream Returns

The familiar hum
Of an old routine;
How often it feels
Like returning to a dream.

The slow moments are over fast
And the times gone by quick
Are the ones that seem to last,
And all of it makes perfect sense.

The dream, the dream!
How often is it,
That you repeat a routine
And wonder when you'll wake?

But here's the thing:
You are awake!
For this is what life will bring,
And what living is all about.

Future's Weight

Being pulled down
To the depths of longing;
People will tell you it's passing,
But it's only prolonging,
And I'm starting to drown.

The days ahead
Seem so far away,
While tomorrow is so close;
Keep your chin up, people say,
But that's already been said.

And sometimes I feel
Like there's no escaping the weight;
But maybe that's just it,
The whole point of your fate:
To let the future heal.

Remember to Remember

Remember to Remember;
Something you don't often hear;
But if you stop and think,
The reasoning is quite clear.

We're all caught up in our own lives,
Our own fear and our own joy,
But really, the future we look to,
Is nothing but a decoy.

There are three times we each have;
The past, full of pain and bliss,
The future, an vast and unknown adventure,
The present, what we most often miss.

Remember to Remember;
All the good, all the bad;
The past, present, and future;
All the memories we wish we had.

Remember to Remember.

The Game

Sometimes the best we can do
Is stare down the mountain,
And keep our chin held high;
For we're all in a game of chance,
Our odds each a pie in the sky.

The Next Mountian

Look up at the majestic beauty;
the endless wonder before you!
And realize your solemn duty
To climb the next mountain.

As the sun moseys overhead
And time marches ever onward,
Feel no fear; Forget all dread!
Just climb the next mountain.

Though the slope is steep
And the path may be perilous,
Never waver! Do not weep!
But climb the next mountain.

Even when dawn draws near
And the end seems so far away,
Listen to the hopeful voice you hear,
Telling you to climb the next mountain.

And once you've finally reached the top,
And your body feels success like no other,
Remember that you mustn't stop,
For you still have the next mountain to climb.

Puzzle Pieces

When chaos seems like the world's natural state,
(It is, but that's not the point of this)
There's no reason for you to wait;
Just adjust your angle to see what you missed.

Often times problems just need a new
perspective
In order to discover the obvious solution.
And you'll find that it's quite effective
At sending demons to their execution.

The demons of time and space
Of many a thought and a dream
(Often metaphorical in this case)
Are often less than they seem.

Simply alter your point of view,
And the puzzle pieces fall into place,
And the world no longer seems askew;
Some order that you can now embrace.

The Hood

The Hood comes on,
Cutting off periphery,
And casting a shadow
Over the heart of thee.

The Hood stays on,
And I slowly start to wonder
If something is wrong,
If your joy has been torn asunder.

The Hood becomes your face,
Covers a gaze surely no longer there,
Taking you miles away from me.
It's almost too much to bear.

But then the Hood comes off.
And your smile tells me
That you just had battles to fight;
And now you're free.

A Little Dose of Empathy

It's a weird experience
Being suddenly shoved
Into the shoes of another,
Like looking at your own reflection
From the mirror's perspective.

You feel odd, jittery,
Like a soul that's wandered too long,
Or as if you're the itch that can't be scratched,
And wonder how you could have
Spent so long in your own head.

But soon enough,
The dust begins to settle,
And you realize the point:
It's not about how you feel.
In fact, it was never about you at all.

Just as it should be.

Life's Blade

You don't realize how often you use it
Until the blade becomes dull
And no longer can you trek through life the
same.

An Old Feeling

An old photograph, sitting on a dresser,
A memory of which you are the sole possessor;
Faces full of meaning, gazing back through time
Smiling in a moment that was truly sublime.
An old feeling.

A familiar place, your presence long gone,
Flashbacks that seem to go on and on;
A thought of how long it's been,
And how the present became so thin.
An old feeling.

Looking up at now, thinking about then;
An old feeling.

Afraid of the Dark

A joke, told over cups of joy;
Laughing, I turn to my right,
But my smile slowly fades:
No one else stands in sight.

I get up, assuring myself,
That everything is alright.
And as I begin to walk away,
A soul becomes less bright.

My mind gets to work,
Choosing which feelings to smite,
And which memories to discard;
The day turns to night.

They say that darkness
Is only the absence of light;
But being afraid of the Dark
Is something only for children, right?

I am not afraid of the Dark,
Or, at least, not quite;
I reel back because I deserve better,
Not because of fright.

Do not be afraid of the Dark,
But do not be afraid to let in the Light.

Harbinger of the Change

The water, shifting underfoot,
Obeys no laws nor counsel,
Moving as the future demands,
The Harbinger of the Change.

The waves that soar high,
Crashing down upon the past,
Only seek to serve
The order among the chaos.

The trench of destiny,
That all must sink down to,
Is the only hope
That the change is real.

The Serpent

Sometimes the serpent is clever,
Pushing you to act and speak
In ways that change you forever.
And the serpent chooses whether
It's good or bad.

But the serpent is not evil,
As some people will claim.
It is merely primeval;
A force of nature,
A piece of you.

The serpent will lash out
With venom of poisoned fury,
Yet also wander about,
Acting with tenderness and warmth,
Barely batting an eye.

Often the serpent will overpower
Your mind, dismissing all logic,
And wholly refusing to cower
To what you know is right.
The serpent feasts; it feels.

And every stoic thought
Or reasonable idea
Counts for naught
As the serpent achieves its goal:
To feel.

Slaying the serpent cannot be done,
And many have given up trying.
But the serpent has not won.
It cannot, so long as we hold on
To the fact that it cannot control us.

Our feelings, of love and of hate,
Need not be listened to at all;
Becoming the serpent is not our fate.
The serpent may be powerful,
But we shouldn't carry its weight.

Step Back

Isn't it just lovely to see
What was, is, and will be?

Priorities

Unfortunately, in life's grand collection of
choices,
There are always many paths, and many voices,
Yet often you can only choose one to take.
And sometimes it seems that no matter which
one you choose
There's always something you have to lose;
Something gained, something lost.
But the choice is still up to you.

www.ingramcontent.com/pod-product-compliance
Lightning Source LLC
Chambersburg PA
CBHW061329140726
47998CB00007B/2616